My Life As An Island

Travis Mossotti

moon city press
springfield missouri

Cover art: "Hills" by Josh Mossotti

ISBN: 978-0-913785-42-3

Interior pages designed by Ethan T. Prince

Moon City Press
Department of English
215 Siceluff Hall
Missouri State University
901 South National
Springfield, MO 65897

www.mooncitypress.com

Acknowledgments:

Big Muddy
"Dupo"

Copper Nickel
"Marizibill"

Italian Americana
"Where We Are Going"

Manchester Review
"Hills"

New South
"My Life As An Island"

Poet Lore
"I Had The Courage..."

River Styx
"Trends Motel"

Southeast Review
"Superior Oak Ridge Landfill"

Water~Stone Review
"If We Are Human Then Let Us Be Fools"

"Trends Motel" was awarded honorable mention for the 2011 *River Styx* International Poetry Prize by contest judge B.H. Fairchild.

Particular gratitude goes out to Rodney Jones, Kerry James Evans, Mark J. Brewin and James Crews for their mentorship and/or camaraderie; to Lanette Cadle and the Moon City Press Poets Council-- Marcus Cafagña, Jane Hoogestraat, and Sara Burge; to Ethan Prince for his work as Design Editor; to my brother Josh for his collaborative workshops and his beautiful art, including the cover for this chapbook; and to my wife Regina and daughter Cora for their love and patience.

For my father and his father

Table of Contents

Between an earth of lovers, these
are the choicest words.
Say them, and they are said.
No one will break his mind on them,
No one in my household.

~George Scarbrough, *Tellico Blue*

Hills

~after Apollinaire

When I stared too long into these Missouri hills,
they curled like slings around broken limbs,
and out came creepers edging the treeline, men with maps,
ancestral black earth, raw childless wind, water.
None of these things were mine. I gave them back

to a minister named Perry, so he might deliver them
from his Sunday pulpit, so he might
find within his open Bible an angel's wing
that holds a place, that holds a passage
from this earth to the next, and he would keep it

for himself. That minister was and will forever
be a fool. He never did represent me
or my country, which I gave back
and found waiting under the same
bridge I crept out from. When I was young,

our cherry tree squirmed its roots towards
China and brought the truly exotic
women within reach. Summer. Noon. I would
fall asleep under the canopy and dream of them.
I imagined their lips were already songs.

Women like that lit fires in the belly
of my father's Buick when it wouldn't
turn over. I watched him lug it from the garage,
beat the hood with a sledge and call it a lousy
American tramp. My father spelled disasters.

You could find him everywhere.
He was like these hills. He towered over
engines that misfired or didn't fire at all.
He knew the mechanics of anger
and frustration because his life

was complete and adorned with roadways
that led him to upper management.
I found it nonsensical, chose instead to let
a few musicians show me the true meaning
of a fifth of bourbon and a barstool

too far from any rocky coast to conjure
an ocean, this river had to suffice.
Stack-O-Lee shot Billy Lyons next to it.
Down near Morgan Street. He didn't shoot him
over a Stetson or cards. It was politics.

And then I became a man, and acted like one.
I followed his trail to the city to find or buy love
somewhere in the music that boomed
from the stacks of steamboats
broken on the Mississippi's filthy shore.

I crossed over one night and came back
married to my own desires, which meant
I'd found the strip clubs and drank all night.
Someone called out the river's depth
as I passed over, and it began to rain.

The city tucked itself under its wing.
A barge dredged for constellations
in the water, and the youthful deities
of wine and dance got covered in it,
plastered in river sludge from head to foot.

I got into my car and turned away
from the sunrise toward the hills and ruins
of a speakeasy. Nothing left but a stone chimney.
Castlewood, Missouri. Al Capone sought refuge
when he was this way, heading for those

always distant hills, and soon the time came
when even I had to pull over and shake
the stink of stripper from my jacket.
I felt like a big Italian woman. My great great
grandmother beating Sienna from her rugs

till its dust swelled in her lungs and she tasted
all the misfortune and suffering to come.
Even my death hovered in her sloppy arm
before it swooped and landed another blow.
Her veins, which were bluer than any river,

became a river worth living next to. That woman
never felt useless or outmoded a day in her life.
One morning, I went to grab the paper and minister Perry
was waiting outside chanting snakes. He lured me
to a fishing boat and set me into the river.

This is God's river, he said. *Your heritage is
as holy and wet as the noses of catfish under
this skiff.* I lowered my hat brim and watched two
squirrels scramble loose from oak branch
to maple and back for almost an hour,

one of them caught up in the rush of wanting
to be on top of the other. I busted the sun
peeking and smelled honeysuckle drifting
from the ether. It reminded me of those Chinese
women under the cherry tree singing

on the other side of the earth, in silk,
in clouds of red silk, and that's when I knew
I loved my father but could never replicate
his body. His back was as tall as a hill
rising to meet a red-tailed hawk

for breakfast. I felt his hands touch
my shoulders as gently as he touched
anything in his entire life, and although I cannot
understand the certitude of cosmologies,
I know that I was born late and frail.

My star hovered over the water at night
then sank under its unbearable weight.
I waved goodbye to the ghosts
of my childhood and married a woman
who was better than jasmine on my tongue.

She took me to a peasant's Paris to float
on the Seine, which was not my river,
which was not my cathedral or carnival feast.
There is no Mediterranean I can't absolve
with a garland of soot, thorn and backwater.

The church bells said goodbye and waved
the way an old man once shook out his hanky
to wipe the tears from the cheek of his bride,
my mother, her mother and every mother
who has borne a body of water that went

nowhere and stank brighter than the halos
of angels. My wife Regina came to understand.
She is the single sweetness I have tasted
and not turned bitter from, the tasting, fell
as a meteorite onto the string of the guitar

a Creole man with four fingers played.
His eyes were closed. He didn't know I was there.
He didn't know his harmonies sizzled in dry grass,
but he halted just the same and sipped an oyster
clean from its shell down to the gullet.

Later, a six-foot snake slipped into the graveyard
at my grandfather's funeral, climbed a tree, wound
its body around a branch and ate robin eggs
out of the nest, one at a time. It might have been
that guitar player. The eggs probably tasted

of freshwater oysters, and Perry's church choir
sang about a shopkeeper who never dies,
who only counts his stock and dusts
his shelves and waits patiently for the time
of burning grace to descend.

Their music scattered like seed. I listened
to the distant barge traffic curdle and knew
I could never leave home, even if I wanted to.
Regina and I watched that minister
bury my grandfather at our feet

in a pit on a hill with a black snake run up
the tree like the flag of this country.
He sermonized an afterlife without peril.
Afterwards, we walked a mile through blight
and found a hawk on a dumpster behind the Chinese

restaurant. It was still morning, but we could smell
last night's braised pork hanging from its beak.
To him, we were no bother.
His head dipped in and out of plastic bags
like a torch that can't be extinguished.

We settled into a cantina booth a few blocks
up the road. The footsteps of the waitress
startled me, and I felt I was being over dramatic.
Like how my father waited years for the mechanic's
whiskered prognosis, timing belt, thermostat

housing, sway bar, junkyard. The dead
abdicate these small privileges and disintegrate.
The gastronomy of hills takes over.
I ordered what passed for huevos rancheros
and went to the bathroom.

Pissing on that blue urinal cake felt nothing like Greece.
I never was a supplicant to Achilles.
My education was public.
The Mississippi creased the back of my country
like the spine of an open book titled *patriotism*.

I never fought pigeons for scraps to call breakfast,
never plucked the whites out of a man's eyes
in new issue boots. I daydreamed women
underneath a cherry tree, traversed
the glory of blue afternoon skies,

was tricked by a minister at the river,
waded into the current to be baptized.
There, knee deep in bilge, all my shortcomings
were forgiven, my doom made certain.
Nothing miraculous can be forestalled.

My father became the glorious red-tailed hawk
on the edge of a rancid dumpster, the twentieth century.
Still, he square danced with my mother every Saturday
when someone booked a caller, drifted
from the dance floor into an orchard

and conceived a family on a bed of constellations,
the streaming hair of apple trees, while all those men
and women who danced simply faded from the planet.
Funny. Our kitchen table had a pine veneer. My father
polyurethaned three extra coats.

It was like staring at a felled tree in a shallow bend
in the river every time we sat down to pray. All of this
I'm remembering now, at a desk, peeling an orange
as the universe gets its virginity back to lose again
during the next meteor shower.

We may be reborn like this, although most of us
end up mounted to the wall in a museum like a dull axe,
as forgotten and worthless as a coin buried in the hillside,
our bodies cursed or filled with baptismal light.
Only invisible things are worth weeping for.

When I was young I thought words like majesty
had a purpose and were not just decorations
for the divinely inbred, but I have been wrong
about many things. I held my wife by the tail end
in the elevator going up to our honeymoon suite,

and she had a current stronger than any Mississippi.
The clerk at the desk brought us ice in the morning.
A few years later we lost a week in a Parisian hostel.
It was abstract. The lost time boiled off as vapor.
Light streamed around her, changed her. Not holy.

The river wasn't holy. Nobody I knew would've dared
to eat a fish out of it. Not my father,
until he became a hawk and gleamed,
and I don't know much about Apollinaire,
other than how I imagine him, looking into the Seine

and thinking about the things that remain, weeping
for the things that disappear. I was dramatic
about my country once and tried to give it back
to some minister with his angel feather
tucked in a Bible that would get him to heaven,

and the Creole guitar player I listened to
at an oyster bar the night I met my wife became
a snake in a cemetery tree eating robin eggs,
became an omen or the flag of my country
or both.

I'm tired of retelling the story of the cosmos
one hill, one river, one sloppy-armed great great
Italian grandmother at a time. I laugh,
and a sunset overtakes me, closes me down.
The natural world is full of this arrogance,

therefore I'm full of arrogance,
with my minor secrets,
my small history rotting me from the inside out,
my sun stalled over the Missouri hills where
my father's Buick has finally rolled to a stop.

My only advice is not to go away,
Or, go away. Most
Of my decisions have been wrong.
        ~Larry Levis, *Winter Stars*

Where We Are Going

In this, the thirtieth year of my life
on earth, I look back on my heritage,
which is the crumbled red brick façade

of burned-out warehouses on the edge
of a river that is more American
than I can stand. The men in my

family grow quiet each Christmas when
salamini and cabbage, a peasant's dish,
goes round the table, and our old Torino

becomes a red wine that soaks up nothing.
It's easy to believe that something sacred
has been lost. It has. It's easy

to lean against the headstone of a grave
that waits to be filled with your body
in a cemetery that nobody visits more

than once and say that we are not where
we have been but where we are going.
Perhaps this too is a lie. My only birthright

is the Mississippi rising and falling
against a St. Louis that was built
with a brass note that escaped the mouth

of a trumpet and traveled to New Orleans,
where the current slowed to a glass of ice
and bourbon and quickly disappeared.

If We Are Human Then Let Us Be Fools

I.

If my father had told me the secret
I'd pass it on now.

Instead,
I'm just another abandoned zinc mine
in the middle of the country,

gladiolas on my wife's Sunday dress,
liver spot on the left wrist

of the dead bartender
who baptized me five nights a week
for nearly ten years. I was devout.

My father told me not to hoot with owls.
My father told me to soar with eagles.

I ordered chicken wings and called it
a compromise.

Even if he hadn't been off hopping
from city to city
selling kitchen implements,

even if he had been a fixture
on the couch each weekend:
lazy bastard, womanizer, creep—

anything. My father told me
that dedication and spite
were tributaries emptying into the same river.

My father told me that love was just an axe
that can't chop wood for shit.

II.

Because you've failed to notice the orchards
dropping their bayonets each autumn,

you've come here for advice.
If we are human then let us be fools.

Let us keep turning to each other
like children
pausing for answers to questions that always begin

and end with why. When winter comes,
you'll know it's your wife's birthday.
When spring shows up, buy it a drink.

Spend the summer watching a field of wheat
fill its golden lungs
with soil.

III.

He stares out from a hotel
towering some strange city

and thinks of his wife
and children. He follows

the smokestacks littering
the industrious part of town

all the way up until they hit
clouds and begin to dream.

He recalls what his father
told him and feels the metal

in his chest grow brittle.
He sinks back into starched

linens and disappears each
night, just like that.

I Had The Courage...

~after Apollinaire

but sold it for a beam of sunlight knifing
a hillside church in two.
It was like splitting an orange
to discover a gold coin
that a woman once choked on
while singing an ode to immortality.
Now, I can't recall much of my childhood,
or the ghosts I emptied
from the Mississippi into that body
of saltwater waiting at its mouth.
I have sold off so much, gotten back
so little in return.

Dupo

~for Levi and Conner

Every day I ended up on the wrong side of the river
heading in the wrong direction, past Dupo, a town slumped
in red brick, tinseled with power lines and blown out
truck tires. Inside there was a bar, Eddie's Place, place
that severed sunlight from day with blacked out windows,

place where inside men could wreck themselves blind
between shifts, if they were working at all, keeping everything
that was broken hidden on the inside—hidden, until two kids
walked in out of nowhere, racked the pool balls and broke
on a table that'd been quiet for years, drank their fill and left.

Their intrusion was no small offense, even if the kids couldn't
have possibly known that some dust was meant to settle
for good, and that those men were, despite their longings,
too egalitarian to have taken issue. I only know this story because
the kids told it to me afterwards—confessed to skipping lecture,

my lecture, for pool and draft beer at three in the afternoon.
I didn't miss them. Maybe because they reminded me of me
at a crossroads when I was their age, and because I knew
what waited outside was only the finest bright silica dust
wafting in from the quarry across the highway, and that towns

like theirs were good for burying people
but not much else. I remember seeing a migrating flock
of red-winged blackbirds resting on Dupo's dense weave
of power lines—the birds must've numbered in the thousands
because every inch of cable for miles was a feathered

red and black boa leading to the Diamond Cabaret,
and clear in the distance loomed St. Louis with its Arch,
and riverboat casinos. If I had squinted hard enough
it might've looked like the city was made of gold,
blessed in sun, as if each building was a saint

waiting to be canonized: patron city of worn thin,
of the levee wall, of the boarded up and ready-to-be
bulldozed warehouses stippled with graffiti. They were
no longer buildings, only the fragile skeletons of the men
who built them, left them to crumble into a Mississippi

they must have dreamed was theirs, a small part of it at least,
dams laid up and downstream for power and commerce.
Last week someone reeled in a giant catfish while fishing
at the Melvin Price Lock and Dam only to watch it die
on its way to the aquarium. The beastly

blue catfish was set to be put on display, but the thing
had grown unnaturally large in the darkness, old white flesh,
sagging blind eyes, the depth making it both strong
and vulnerable, like all myth, and when I told my students
in attendance that the fish was not a fish but the body

of Walter S. Powell, a local St. Louis businessman,
whose name was struggling to remain attached to the city,
they only believed in the man, not the fish, because
they weren't drunk enough or sad or lonely enough yet
to cross that river—not like the boys back in Dupo

shooting pool on a table that wasn't level and leaned
each shot toward the same corner pocket. Three pitchers
deep, they probably got fed up with the dregs at the bar
who'd been channeled into a dark and pitiful silence,
must have noticed the broken window letting in a furious pillar

of light and felt the overlap of desire and need, fact
and myth. When they left it must have been like walking
into a fog, dust billowing from the quarry into Eddie's
graveled lot—gravel that used to be a bluff a man
once stood on the edge of and pulled himself back from.

There is a river we are meant to cross only once,
but it's not this one: not this Mississippi, this channel
of commerce stuck in its wide course, this floodplain,
this silo rotting in a field of artificial corn, this quarry
chunking the limestone bluffs into meaningless piles of chert.

Trends Motel
~Ellisville, MO

Each year I come home to visit my
family, and the one sleazy motel
with its flickering neon vacancy
still stands. And I can remember
the discarded old men I worked
with each summer, consummate
lifelong losers all, who lived out
of station wagons and pick-ups
during the week, the same men
who kept the few hookers in town
busy, so they could bring to work
on Mondays their meager triumphs,
their money well spent. It's likely
those men are in jail by now or dead,
and this place with its paybythehour
motif serves as the only reminder
that they ever even existed. Perhaps
if I stayed here a single night, under
the miserable sagging white ceilings
where they looked for answers
to questions they must've known
were meaningless, like their lives,
perhaps I could empathize a little
with what it means to live on
the wrong side of mercy, although
I doubt it. I doubt I'd find more than
a blade of grass left from a boot sole
of a drifter keeping warm in a Buick
in some other state, because after all,
this is still America, a county so big
it's no wonder some of us get lost.

Marizibill

~after Apollinaire

The Ozark lake where she grew is wrecked
with the pallor of winter and out-of-work
Johns, with slow boats, with houses pecked
clean of families. Trifles of smoke and sex
littered the bar where I once sifted ore

in whiskey and ice. She was the dartboard
that locals took shots at, nailed, and became
nothing more than imagined air in this crude
place, a smear of brass rail moored to the bar's
lip, a dartboard's smooth and untouched frame.

My Life As An Island

"No man is an Island, entire of itself; every man
is a piece of the Continent, a part of the main."
~John Donne, Meditation XVII

I.

When we crossed over the Mississippi
the city pricked up like an electric fence,

and a casino billboard said that, *Elvis Lives
five nights a week,* while the water beneath us

blackened silently. My wife's sister's husband
fell in with another woman the night prior,

fingered off those pink dainties to hang
on a hotel doorknob, called room service

in the morning, and couldn't just leave
well enough alone—then it became our problem.

And so we crossed over from Illinois to help
change the locks, a sort of commissioned

moral support in case he came home drunk,
indignant, trying his lame key

under the porch light. But he never did.
Nothing happened. Instead he lumbered in

to a motel, slept it off, woke up
with a hangover and went to work.

Our lives brimmed with the anti-climax
of his single night spent sleeping alone

in the spoon position.
In the morning, they decided to reconcile.

II.

Somehow I'd fallen asleep by the door that night
and dreamed I turned into a stone carving

on Easter Island. Stoic. All primal
forehead and black volcanic rock.

Islanders kept leaving wreathes of flowers,
and a few times I saw his truck

idling by the mailbox—only, I couldn't
make him out, couldn't be sure that I was even

awake. But then I listened as his foot
kept thudding against the brass kick plate,

rhythmic as empty train cars pushing
north to the coal pits, night tucked

like a sharp knife in his boot.
It had grown crowded with statues,

and my father sat next to me to watch
the wind clip the heads off breakers.

He said that meditation like this was for
cowards: *a man's got to know his place.*

Together we watched the sun float out
beyond the surf on a raft. Light came through

a window, crossed my forehead
and crept inside the smell of butter browning

a skillet. I scratched it off, still in jeans,
and went to the kitchen where she stood in a white

bathrobe spreading butter, cigarette
in her free hand, asked if I slept at all.

Where's my wife, I said.

III.

There's no hope of prosthesis for a failing marriage.
It simply rots and falls off.

IV.

When the dust had altogether settled
around my wife's sister's husband,

our presence no longer needed,
we drove home to Illinois and all

of the lovesick buzzards came out
to welcome us. They gathered around

the cracked belly of a deer carcass
that'd painted a stripe of itself

across the highway—
each bird bowing its blood covered

head as though it were a monk
robed in feathers, lost in meditation.

Travis Mossotti teaches English at Lindenwood University, and his poetry has appeared in such places as the *Antioch Review*, *Manchester Review*, *Prairie Schooner*, *Poetry Ireland Review*, *Southwest Review*, *The Writer's Almanac*, *Verse Daily*, *Western Humanities Review* and many others. Mossotti was awarded the 2011 May Swenson Poetry Award by contest judge Garrison Keillor for his first collection of poems, *About the Dead* (USU Press, 2011), and in 2010 his poem "Decampment" was adapted to screen as an animated short film. The Sustainable Arts Foundation awarded Mossotti a grant in 2012 in support of a forthcoming collection of poems *Field Study*, and he was also named Poet-in-Residence at the Endangered Wolf Center in St. Louis, Missouri. Mossotti currently resides in St. Louis with his wife Regina and their daughter Cora.